Raccoons

Friendly Bandits!

Dr. Richard A. NeSmith

Love of Nature Series

ISSUE 1

Applied Principles of Education & Learning

APE-Learning

© 2020 Richard A. NeSmith
Love of Nature Series

http://richardnesmith.obior.cc/

All images in this book are copyright by their respective authors.

Dr. Richard A. NeSmith

ISBN: 9798653160264

Oct 2021

FLESCH-KINCAID GRADE LEVEL: 8.2

DEDICATION

This wildlife booklet is the first in a series and is dedicated to **Michael Gardner**, my childhood friend. He had the first pet raccoon I ever encountered. It was gorgeous and made me very curious, but Mike was careful to teach me to respect it, for it was a *wild animal*. I hope you enjoy this booklet filled with facts and fancies of raccoons, the friendly bandits.

ABOUT RACCOONS

Raccoons are native mammals found throughout the United States. It is said that the explorer Christopher Columbus was the first European to write about raccoons. The word ***raccoon*** is a native Powhatan word that means "animal that scratches with its hands." The scientific name is **Procyon**, which similarly means *before dog washer*. So, they are actually named for their use of hands. They use their hands to *see* their environment.

Their hands are some of the most coordinated and nimble of all animals and very quick. Unlike most animals, they actually pick up their food and place it in their mouth instead of leaning over and eating as a dog or cat would do. They can easily hold and manipulate food with their five toes on each paw (which has an opposable thumb) and prefer to wash or moisten their food in water. Wetting their paws seems to heighten the sensitivity of their paws. They are so intelligent and coordinated; they can even open human food containers, coolers, and ice chests. The raccoon has extra sensitive touch/feel organs on the ends of their toes (fingers) that almost act like taste buds. They

help them determine what is edible and what is not. You might say that raccoons are *feeling their food.* It might even be fair to say that these receptors almost act like eyes, as the

raccoon uses its hands to feel for and handle food without looking or needing to see it. They catch a lot of their food by snaring it out of the water. They especially like crayfish and frogs.

There are six different species in the United States. They are common and native

to North and Central America, seeming to differ primarily in size. Though appearing more cat-like in appearance, they are thought to be more genetically related to bears.

They were sought after for their furs in the New World

from 1790-1890. So much so that they became invasive in other parts of the world due to being exported to Europe for fur farming. Raccoons have very soft fur, but the inner underfur is thickest and makes up nearly 90 percent of their coat.

Raccoons are very family-oriented and known to protect their offspring passionately. Though they appear to be very shy but friendly, they are to be respected and given their space. Learn to enjoy them from a distance. Never assume that any wild animal is tame. There is a reason they are called "wild" and make up our wonderful "wildlife." Raccoons, like most wild animals, can be unpredictable and aggressive. They have 40 teeth, which include four long, sharp, canine teeth in front. Their claws are sharp. *Never* corner a raccoon. If you need to remove a raccoon, call a wildlife removalist. They know what to do to avoid injury or to avoid injuring a raccoon.

Remember that a mother raccoon will die for her kits.

They are omnivores, which means *they eat almost anything.* They can wreak havoc on gardens as they love fresh fruits and vegetables. They eat insects, eggs, poultry, rats, squirrels, birds, fish, crawfish, snakes, worms, frogs, mollusks, and even small livestock. If available, they will eat pet food, carrion (dead animals), and human garbage. Some

raccoons raised from birth have been domesticated. Generally, this requires a permit from the state in which one lives. One was even a pet of President Coolidge in the White House long ago.

Raccoons are about the size of a small 8-23 pound dog and are most distinguished for their black mask on white and their bushy-ringed tail. The largest on record was 60 pounds (27 kg)! Some have four stripes on their tails, and others have five. Males are generally larger than females. A raccoon's eyesight is not very good. But the dark "mask" actually serves a purpose other than to make them look like adorable burglars.

The "mask" helps improve vision, though their eyesight is not very good. The dark band reduces glare by absorbing light during bright sunlight, much like the black grease baseball and football players apply during a day game. It also reduces distracting light glare at night outside of the center of view. Their hearing, however, is excellent. That is one reason you do not see most of the raccoons present during your hike because a human's voice often sends them hiding.

They have also been considered one of the smartest animals in the forest, considered just below great apes and monkeys. They are much more intelligent than your dog. Some studies reveal that raccoons can remember solutions or tasks for up to 3 years. In addition, they have been found to copy one another's actions that are beneficial to survival. Though it is said, they can be easily trained, but they are too wild to be contained. They are so curious that they love to explore and can create quite a mess of things, especially if they enter a person's home. They can be quite the trouble-maker and cause havoc. In some cases, they have even entered homes and set up dens.

Though nocturnal (night creature), it is not uncommon to see them out during the day. They are very social and even clean creatures, and where you see one, there is probably another one nearby. Raccoons make over 50 different sounds to communicate, including whistling and purring.

They do seem to sleep mainly during the day. They sleep even more in the winter, often using up stored fat, but they do not hibernate. However, in cold regions, they do experience *torpor* in which the body's metabolism and organs slow down. It is not a true form of hibernation, but close. They can sleep in the torpor state for a week or so before waking to forage for food and water.

Some think the ringed tail's significance is that an attacking predator would be the first thing noticed. So, the tail might

be attacked, leaving the raccoon free to scamper off alive. Raccoons also can turn their heads 180 degrees (most people can only turn their heads 90 degrees left or right!). It has become, with the black-eye mask, the raccoon's trademark.

At one time, it was believed that raccoons always had to dip their food in water because they were missing saliva glands. Biologists have since discovered that they do have saliva glands that work perfectly fine. However, the nature to immerse their food in water is so strong they go through those motions even if water is not present. The practice of

immersing one's food in water is called *dousing* and seems to heighten the sense of touch for the raccoon.

Raccoons prefer heavily wooded environments with access to trees, water, and an abundance of vegetation. However, they seem to have become adapted to nearly any environment and are often thriving in cities.

Some biologists have suggested that urban raccoons are even smarter than country ones due to the obstacles they must overcome to survive in an unnatural environment. In many cities, the large number of raccoon residents is unimaginable. For example, in some parts of Washington, DC, it has been said that raccoons number around 300 per kilometer! Toronto, Canada, may have the largest urban raccoons population than any other place, and has even been called

the "Raccoon capital of the world." There these uber-raccoons are affectionately known as "trash pandas."

The population of raccoons can be 20 times greater in urban areas as compared to rural areas. So, where there is food, there are probably raccoons. In a forest, they make dens in hollow parts of trees or abandoned burrows, such as those of the gopher tortoise. A group of raccoons is called a *gaze*.

Some dens may contain as many as 30 raccoons, although it

is more common to have just four. Their "territory" can

range up to 18 miles, and they mark these with their poop (excrement), with 2-4 inch scat droppings. They are also excellent swimmers.

Though *cute as a button* and often given human-like attributes (called *anthropomorphism*) like attractive, friendly, adorable, and loving, they can become pests. They are problem-solvers and seek to find ways to obtain food that most animals cannot do. Such as

Here I was trying to get this photograph of the raccoon before she scampered off quickly into the brush. I noticed that she refused to make eye contact. R. NeSmith

opening trash cans or putting an item inside a container to raise the water level, making the food reachable.

Veterinarian Dr. Laurie Aleixo has helped rehabilitate many raccoons, including infants (see also her other photos on top of page 20). She states that every raccoon she has ever rehabbed has his/her own personality. They are very trusting in captivity when they know who provides their food.

They have been able to open doors, remove locks, turn bolts, buttons, and climb in or out of boxes. Some make their homes, called dens, in home's attics, and some have even been known to raid the cupboard.

Finally, we must mention that raccoons

are easily susceptible to rabies, a highly contagious disease resulting from a virus that spreads through infected animals' saliva. They are ***primary carriers*** of rabies in the United States, followed by foxes, skunks, and bats. The disease can be spread by being bitten by an infected animal. Rabies can be spread to humans and, though it can be treated, can lead to death. Rabid raccoons are dangerous, for their brains are affected in such a way as to make them hostile and to attack due to the confusion it creates. Rabies' symptoms can include difficulty walking, stumbling, paralyzed hind legs,

Photo by Dr. Laurie Aleixo

confusion,
disoriented,
hurting itself,
unusual noise-
making,
foaming in the
mouth, and
generally

disoriented or sitting without much movement or activity.
Report such animals to your local ranger.[1] Always keep
your distance but especially avoid animals that might seem
to be acting strangely.

Another disease one must consider with raccoons is
roundworms. These are shed in the raccoon's feces (called

---

[1] Or call your county health department or animal control agency with your description and location of the animal.

scat). This parasite can get into the human body and cause diseases of the organs and even the eyes.

Male raccoons are called **boars**, whereas females are referred to as **sows**. Raccoons breed during the winter and early spring. Most raccoon babies are born in spring (March/April), and there are 3 to 5 in a litter, though there can be up to 7. Baby raccoons are called kits (or cubs) often spend the first two months in the den. They are born blind and deaf and develop these senses during the third week of life. They are weaned from their mother's milk around 2-4 months. At 12 weeks, they venture out of the den and begin roaming and searching for food entire nights with their mother.

Because young raccoons are still susceptible to predators, the mother will have several hiding places for her young,

should danger occur. Within 8 to 12 months, they become independent and eventually set out on their own. When a raccoon feels threatened by an attacker, they will generally run away or climb a tree. Because their front legs are shorter than their hind legs, a raccoon appears to hunch over when walking or running.

Raccoons can run up to 15 mph (24 km/h) and, it has been reported that they can fall 35 to 40 feet (11 to 12 meters) without injury. Unlike most mammals, raccoons can climb or run down a tree headfirst by rotating their hind feet 180 degrees. Raccoons typically live for 2 to 3 years in the wild. The oldest raccoon on record lived in captivity to be 22 years of age. They do not have many natural predators, but a large number are killed yearly by automobiles. Bobcats, coyotes, wolves, panthers, and hawks have all been known

to attack them.

Remember that when dealing with wild animals, including raccoons, "cute" is a human perception we bestow upon them and one that is entirely subjective.

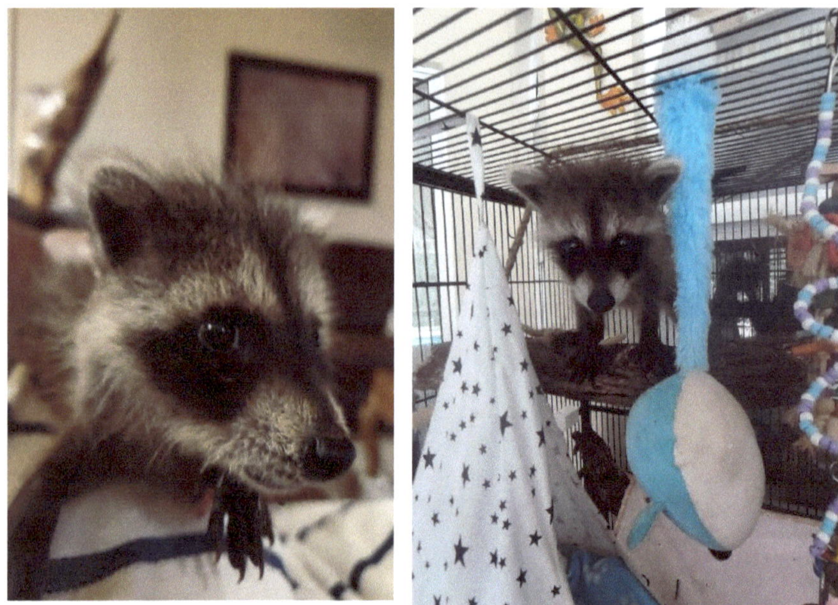

Photos by Dr. Laurie Aleixo

A group of *baby* raccoons is called a *nursery,* a single baby is a *kit* or *cub.*

From the photos below, one can appear so cute and cuddly and yet very dangerous in a split moment of time.

In considering raccoons, we have found they are beautiful

and admirable animals found throughout the United States. They are very successful in surviving in natural environments and urban areas where people and food are abundant. If you are in a park and see a raccoon, then stop and watch and admire it. There is no need to fear it. But, never feed it (or any other wildlife), because doing so will cause them to lose their fear of humans, which is when they become dangerous. Most animals fear humans, and that brings with it safety for both the animal and people.

Raccoons are, indeed, friendly bandits. Let's keep it that way.

REVIEW

1. What does the name "raccoon" actually mean?

2. What kind of diet do raccoons have?

3. Why are raccoons so successful, even in the midst of expanding human neighborhoods?

4. How does the raccoon's "mask" help it survive?

5. What does it mean that we often speak of animals anthropomorphically?

6. What disease are raccoons most susceptible to?

7. What should you do if you see a rabid raccoon?

RACCOON

COLORING PAGE

http://clipart-library.com/clipart/19-6Tp5Xg6TE.htm

Raccoons!

Complete the crossword puzzle below

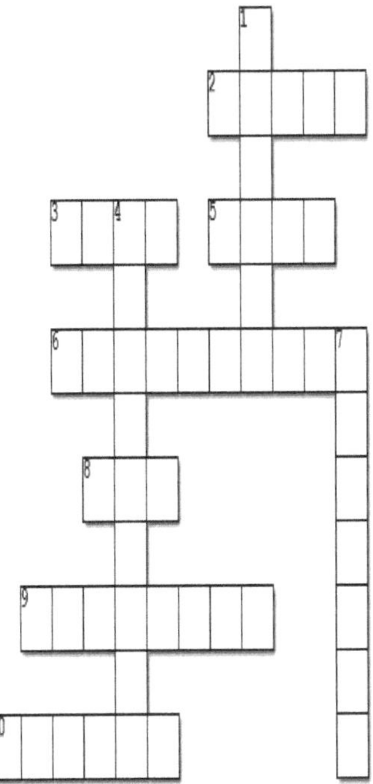

Created using the Crossword Maker on TheTeachersCorner.net

Across

2. That which seems to be the reason for the name 'raccoon'?
3. That which helps remove glare
5. How many toes does a raccoon have on a foot?
6. What is one sign of a rabid raccoon?
8. Name for a baby raccoon
9. What is it called when an animal can nearly eat any kind of food?
10. What kind of environments do raccoons prefer?

Down

1. What disease are raccoons known as primary carriers?
4. What is extra special about raccoon's fingers?
7. Group of baby raccoon

INTERESTING SOURCES TO CONSIDER:

20 Amazing Facts About Raccoons. Available at:
   https://youtu.be/IpfIfOS-OiM

Amazing Facts About Raccoons. Available at:
   https://youtu.be/jrONMGHK66o

Everything You Need To Know About Raccoons Revealed!!! Available at:
   https://youtu.be/rO8jxovWdQ0

Everything You Need to Know about Raccoons: Westchester, NY: Intrepid Wildlife Services. Available at: https://youtu.be/-qiiO31CN-o

Interesting Facts about Raccoons: Cute Animal Video for School Learning. National Geographic Documentary Available at: https://youtu.be/L8xe9XSQvQw

Raccoon. Amazing Animals. Amazing Animals. National Geographic Kids. Available at:
   https://youtu.be/1lViKrWgTYk

Raccoon's Secret Superpower. Available at:
   https://youtu.be/Bre19eDilZU

ABOUT THE AUTHOR

Richard NeSmith is a native of Florida, USA. He grew up wading through the swamps of central Florida with his two younger brothers during the pre-Disney era and unknowingly fell in love with biology, wildlife, and nature. He has lived in seven American states, twice in Australia and once in Mexico City. He holds eight university degrees and has taught for 14 years in secondary schools, here and abroad, and another 13 years as a professor in several American universities. His service includes professor of science education, Dean of Education, Campus Dean, and an online instructor. His passion for learning (and *how we learn*) did not develop until *after* graduating from high school. His only explanation for this is that *having a goal made all the difference in the world*. He enjoys reading, hiking, nature photography, golf, and tennis.

Educational, wildlife, and naturalist books
Dr. Richard NeSmith.

Applied Principles of Education & Learning

APE-Learning

Available on Amazon.com at
http://amazon.com/author/richardnesmith

Website: http://richardnesmith.obior.cc

Applied **P**rinciples of **E**ducation & Learning *presents*

https://amzn.to/325p92Y

AMAZON AUTHOR's PAGE:

https://www.amazon.com/author/richardnesmith

e-books: https://bit.ly/3iuCgB3

Issue 1
Raccoons:
Friendly Bandits
Dr. Richard NeSmith

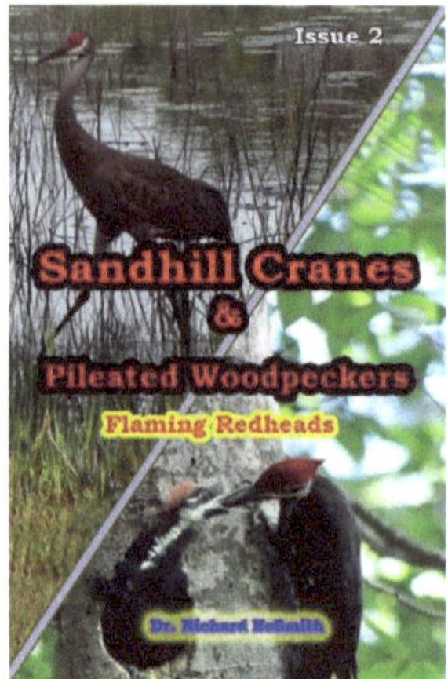
Issue 2
Sandhill Cranes
&
Pileated Woodpeckers
Flaming Redheads
Dr. Richard NeSmith

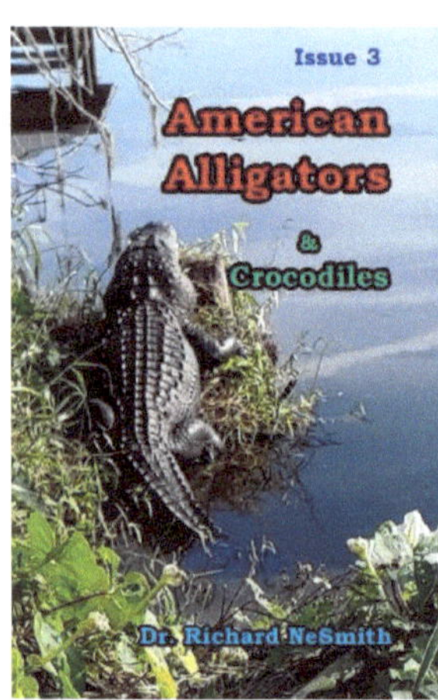
Issue 3
American
Alligators
&
Crocodiles
Dr. Richard NeSmith

Issue 4
Bobcats:
Ghostly Elusive
Dr. Richard NeSmith

Issue 5
Foxes:
Sneaky Rascals
Dr. Richard NeSmith

Issue 6
Armadillo:
Little Armored One
Dr. Richard NeSmith

Issue 7
Squirrels:
Bushy Tail Scampers
Dr. Richard NeSmith

Issue 8
River Otters:
Aquatic Clowns!
Dr. Richard NeSmith

Issue 9
Beavers:
Nature's Engineers !
Dr. Richard NeSmith

Issue 10
Black Bears
Titans of the Forest
Dr. Richard NeSmith

Issue 11
Freshwater
Turtles
Dr. Richard NeSmith

Issue 12
FUNGI, LICHENS
& MUSHROOMS
Dr. Richard NeSmith

NEW: *Love of Nature* Series ISSUES 1-10 in a single volume! $ave 50% off
363-pages/ enhanced / full-color

https://bit.ly/3d83m0T

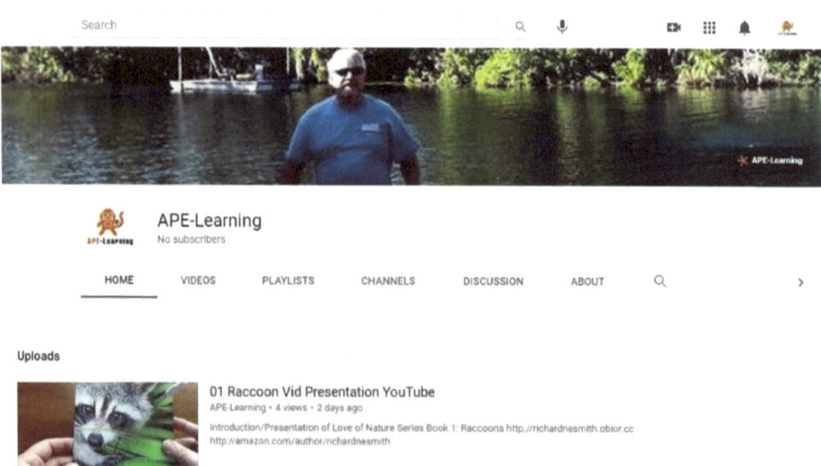

Love Learning – Love Nature – Love Life